IS BASEBALL HOLY?

IS BASEBALL HOLY?

JACK KEROUAC and THE NATIONAL PASTIME

GREGORY STEPHENSON

Ober-Limbo Verlag

Grateful acknowledgement is made to Gary Cieradkowski for permission to use the illustration appearing on the cover, taken from *The League of Outsider Baseball: An Illustrated History of Baseball's Forgotten Heroes* by Gary Cieradkowski (Attica Books, 2015) and to Bill Staples, Jr. for permission to reproduce the image appearing on page 12, taken from his blog *international pastime*.

Published by Ober-Limbo Verlag
Heidelberg, Germany

ISBN 978-87-971569-5-7

Cover design & layout: Birgit Stephenson

For Birgit,
persistent genius

*"Baseball is a universe as large as life
itself, and therefore all things in life,
whether good or bad, whether tragic
or comic, fall within its domain."*
-- Paul Auster

"Is baseball holy?"

With the resonance of a zen koan, the question is left hanging midair in the mind. "Peter the saint" asks it of "the Bishop" in Jack Kerouac's text for the film, *Pull My Daisy.* [1] "Is baseball holy?" Peter inquires of the shy, dignified clergyman seated before him on a sofa. Disconcerted, the Bishop declines to answer, remaining silent. What Peter seems to imply by his question is whether the concept of holiness might not be extended to encompass activities conventionally considered to be unconcerned with religion or religious purposes. And, more specifically, is the game of baseball of such a nature as to be regarded – either in whole or in part – as sacred or spiritual in character? The eager, unaffected manner with which Peter poses the question would seem to suggest that he himself believes this to be the case.

Though Peter's question may at first seem so, it is neither impertinent nor absurd, and is, indeed, one that has in the years since *Pull My Daisy* first flickered on the screens of art house cinemas been pondered and plumbed by several scholars of religion and of sport, all of whom affirm that the game of baseball possesses a spiritual essence or spiritual dimension. Before addressing the motif of baseball in Kerouac's writings, then, I will present a brief survey of reflections on this issue as made by a range of authors.

George Grella, for example, argues that with its seasonal rhythms and rituals "the magical qualities of primitive religion also exist in baseball," whose life-giving powers may be seen to hold at bay from spring to autumn, "the forces of death, darkness and sterility." [2] The game is, Grella asserts, "a sport that partakes of the divine and the transcendent." [3] Arguing along similar lines, Michael L. Butterworth states that baseball "commands religious respect because its rituals and symbols manifest an underlying mythology that should be called religious." [4] In a like manner, Gary Laderman discerns a "spirituality embedded in the game," in that baseball "embodies lessons about values and morality, can lead to experiences that are pivotal and transformative, and provides an avenue for transcendence." [5]

In an article titled "A Perfect Game: The Metaphysical Meaning of Baseball," David Bentley Hart contends that baseball is the expression of a Platonic perfect game (an ideal form existing in eternity.) [6] Hart advances the argument that baseball with its innate philosophical and metaphysical implications ("departure from and ultimate return to an abiding principle") its mystic proportions, its pathos, its contemplative aspects and its sheer purity of action, must be seen to constitute a "philosophical grammar" that is unmistakably Platonist in nature. Moreover, Hart asserts, the game is "certainly religious through and through." [7]

The title of John Sexton's study of baseball and spirituality, *Baseball as a Road to God,* states clearly the book's thesis. [8] Sexton argues that there are significant parallels between baseball and religion, including rituals and ceremonies, sacred times and sacred spaces, informing myths, faith, miracles, blessings and the conversion experience. But the author believes that baseball is more than merely a civil or secular religion. Sexton finds that, in common with spiritual traditions, "baseball has the capacity to elevate and transform" both individuals and communities. [9] It has, he declares, the potential to "give us a sense of the ineffable, the transcendent." [10] The attention, devotion and faith a fan or a player brings to the game of baseball, the author maintains, can serve to stimulate and enlarge their capacity to discover and respond to the sacred more generally. In this sense – properly apprehended – baseball may be understood as evoking in its followers and participants "the essence of religion. " [11]

In his penetrating study, *Baseball Metaphysics,* Daniel McNeil perceives in the National Pastime parallels to broader aspects of American life, including issues of individual freedom and free enterprise. A deeper, more essential pattern underlying the game of baseball, though, is seen by the author as that of the Christian mystery of Fall and Redemption. In dramatic form, McNeil maintains, baseball expresses the stages of the foundational Christian narrative: "a primary state of innocence, the batter setting himself at the plate; a temptation, the offering of the pitcher; a fall, the self-condemnation by hitting to the diminished role of base-runner; sin, the passive touching of a base; faith, running the bases or taking a daring lead off base; grace, a sudden aid that leads to advancement along the base paths, or to scoring; and the final redemption of reaching the place where the player was at the beginning." [12] A baseball game may thus be seen as a form of Christian allegory, a kind of improvised Miracle Play with eighteen actors.

Baseball: "it's the golden metaphysics of life itself, focused on a field of play," pronounces Marvin Cohen in his lively and acute, analytical and poetical exposition of the game, *Baseball as Metaphysics.* [13] Baseball is, Cohen further asserts, "an experience encircled by every overtone of existence," comprehending such fundamental principles as truth, order, mystery and beauty. [14] The game is viewed by Cohen as sharing with religion the capacity to catalyze in its devotees epiphanies and "transcendent transports" of consciousness. [15] Epiphanies that transform commonplace awareness into "a new, perhaps keener, version of reality," verging on a species of revelation. [16] Transcendent transports that momentarily release the mind from its prison of self-conscious selfhood and simultaneously both satisfy and tantalize the human hunger for metaphysical meaning: "That all-embracing electricity that fires up everyone to be stirred by the same current. A feeling of total Belonging ... that certain key moment that hinted as to the meaning of life. It didn't 'give away' life's mystery, but there sure was an illumination!" [17]

As a further, final bit of lyrical testimony advancing the notion that baseball can be considered to instantiate spiritual values, there is John Updike's poem, "Tao in the Yankee Stadium Bleachers," which combines allusions to Mickey Mantle and Yogi Berra with allusions to Dante Alighieri, Chuang-tzu and the Inner Journey, finding in the game of baseball affirmations of tenets of the Tao. [18]

Image courtesy of Bill Staples, Jr.

Though, I cannot, of course, make any claim to speak on behalf of Jack Kerouac, I am inclined to believe that he would have pronounced himself well pleased with certain of the arguments advanced by the above-named authors. What is clear from Kerouac's writings on baseball is that he saw in the sport vital values and meanings profoundly significant to the human spirit. Baseball was for him, as I hope to show, a "sacred space" – a solace and a sanctuary, a source of insight and inspiration, a lost Eden and a promise of Paradise.

Readers of Kerouac's novels *Doctor Sax* (1959) and *Desolation Angels* (1965) will recall the author's descriptions of his elaborate self-invented fantasy baseball leagues, their teams and seasons. This topic has been admirably treated by Isaac Gewirtz in *Kerouac at Bat: Fantasy Sports and the King of the Beats,* so I will refrain from discussing it here, except to say that Kerouac's solitary, life-long, ever-unfolding fantasy baseball saga clearly serves to confirm the centrality of the game in his imagination. [19]

The special significance of baseball to Jack Kerouac can also be seen in the frequency with which the author makes reference to the sport or employs it as a motif in his writing. In the following, I would like to take a wide sweeping look at reflections on and representations of baseball in Kerouac's letters, journals, fiction, poetry and essays.

The earliest example from Kerouac's hand of what might be seen as baseball fiction is a piece he wrote at age 16 as a supplement to his fantasy baseball game. Cast in the form of a sports column under the byline of "Jack Lewis," (an anglicized form of Kerouac's name, Jean-Louis) the composition is included in *Atop an Underwood,* Paul Marion's collection of Kerouac's early writings. [20] Marion notes in his commentary to "Jack Lewis's Baseball Chatter" that the piece stands out from the young Kerouac's earlier fantasy baseball writing in that it "opens like a short story and develops into a scene with characters, dialogue, and setting." [21] The theme of the fictional column (an interview by sportswriter Jack Lewis with Bob Chase, manager of the New York Chevvys team) is that of the unpredictable nature of baseball. A single swing of a bat or a single error can change a game. A single game – won or lost – can change the fortunes of a team. Likelihoods, probabilities, the performance and momentum of teams and of individual players can suddenly and radically be altered by chance or by an act of free will. [22] Implicit here is a celebration of the notion that baseball effectively thwarts and refutes determinism while affirming in its stead possibility and human freedom.

All during the course of the interview, the Chevvy's manager persists in flicking apple seeds through the open window of his tenth floor office, out into the spring air. At least one of those seeds may well find a patch of fertile soil and germinate. Perhaps the tender shoot thus created may even one day grow to bear fruit. There is, of course, no certainty that such a course of events will take place, but there is a certainty that the possibility exists. As the Chevvy's manager observes: "anything may happen to anything." [23]

Also included in *Atop an Underwood* is an excerpt from a baseball novella written by young Kerouac, titled "Raw Rookie Nerves." The protagonist of the piece is a rookie second baseman named Freddy Burns who has just been called up to the majors. Intimidated and lacking self-confidence, Burns performance on the field is uneven and for his mistakes he is cruelly badgered by a teammate, a veteran player named Nick Vickers. In the climactic scene of the story, Burns turns on Vickers, and with a well-placed blow knocks him unconscious.

The theme of the piece is the archetypal motif of initiation, the passage of Freddy Burns from awkward adolescent diffidence to a more poised and self-possessed young manhood, a transition achieved through the ordeals he faces and overcomes in playing major league baseball. There may be a sense in which Nick Vickers may be seen as an external embodiment of Burns' own selfconsciousness and self-reproaches. In overthrowing Vickers, the protagonist overthrows those inward weaknesses that impede him in manifesting his latent strengths as a player. A sub-theme of "Raw Rookie Nerves" (as in "Jack Lewis's Baseball Chatter") would seem to be that of the unpredictable nature of the game of baseball. In a key play – one which might have earned the rookie the respect of his team-mates – a "bad hop" by the ball, an unusual and unlikely occurrence, causes Burns to miss a catch and to be charged with an error. Accepting and adjusting to the unforeseeable, he learns, is a key element of the game and a crucial insight into the essential character of life in an uncertain world.

The gloom-dispelling, spirit-lifting, joy-inducing potential of baseball's radical unpredictability is extolled by Kerouac in an entry in his personal journal for October 1951 and again in an essay he wrote some eight years later. Both writings refer to the same inspiring incident, one that is considered to be a notable occasion in baseball history: New York Giants outfielder Bobby Thomson's game-winning, pennant-winning, 9th inning, three-run home run ("the shot heard 'round the world") at the Polo Grounds in Manhattan, New York on October 3rd, 1951.

Kerouac's journal entry for that day portrays the author sunk in dejection, brooding all day over his debts and his lack of prospects, his health and his sense of failure, and a conviction of having wasted his life. "Nothing but shit falling from heaven," he writes in a mood of near despondency. [24] Then, at his brother-in-law's house, he watches on television the crucial National League pennant game.

His own dark mood is matched by that of the Giants fans he observes on the television screen as the decisive game nears its disheartening end: "... a cruel joke now, a thing in the iron breast of laughing time." [25] Even the fading light of an October dusk seems to confirm the end of hope: "The field is dark, the sky is dimming." [26] The dismal final minutes of the now almost-lost game coming after the brave strivings of the Giants for so long a time seems a chain of events exactly parallel to his own sad situation.

Suddenly, with two outs and two men on base, Thomson hits "a miraculous homerun," and soul-souring imminent defeat becomes in an instant soaring joy. A player has defied fate, defied probability, defied every prediction and circumstance and with a single act of will and skill has affirmed human possibility. This dramatic reversal reverberates deep in Kerouac's spirit. "There was," he writes, "the sudden realization that winning is possible on earth." [27]

Eight years later, in an essay titled "On the Origins of a Generation," the inspiriting, odds-conquering, heroic home run by Bobby Thomson again causes Kerouac to rhapsodize and to affirm its significance. [28] Expressing his dismay with and disavowal of a group of "beatniks" who have recently (i.e. 1958) undertaken a public protest against baseball, Kerouac writes of them: "Bunch of fools marching against the San Francisco Giants, as if (now) in my name, and I, my childhood ambition to be a big league baseball star hitter like Ted Williams, so that when Bobby Thomson hit that homerun in 1951 I trembled with joy and couldn't get over it for days and wrote poems about how it was possible for the human spirit to win after all!" [29]

In the same essay, Kerouac explains the circumstances leading to his having named the Beat Generation, and his personal understanding of the word beat, "as being to mean beatific." [30] If, as Kerouac states, to be beat is "the root, the soul of Beatific," [31] then what incident could more dramatically illustrate the sudden transformation of defeat and despair into bliss and blessedness than Bobby Thomson's home run?

Bobby Thomson makes another appearance in Kerouac's writing, in the pages of the author's celebrated novel *On the Road,* in a scene where the narrator, Sal Paradise, and his friend, Dean Moriarty, both eager to engage in life as fully as possible, follow simultaneously three baseball games: "I had a television set. We played one ballgame on the TV, another on the radio, and kept switching to a third and kept track of all that was happening every moment. 'Remember, Sal, Hodges is on second in Brooklyn so while the relief pitcher is coming in for the Phillies we'll switch to Giants–Boston and at the same time notice where DiMaggio has three balls count and the pitcher is fiddling with the resin bag, so we quickly find out what happened to Bobby Thomson when we left him thirty seconds ago with a man on third.' " [32]

Beyond being a source of stimulation and intensity for the narrator of *On the Road,* in one instance in the novel baseball also becomes for him a kind of moral-psychological touchstone, a catalyst for self-examination. As Sal Paradise wanders alone in the streets of Denver one soft spring evening, he comes upon a ballgame played under the lights by two uniformed amateur teams. Witnessing the players of all races – "white, colored, Mexican, pure Indian" – performing on the field with "heart-breaking seriousness," he contrasts their whole-hearted earnestness and eagerness with his own youthful elite-athletic, upwardly-mobile ambitions as a player. He reproaches himself for his former rigid egotism, his "big-time, sober-faced" calculated aspirations, and he envies the simple "boyish human joy" of the teams playing before bleachers filled with cheering spectators, families and friends, young and old, a cross-section of "all humanity." [33] Feeling exiled by his vanity from such innocent enjoy-ments and recognizing that in his former ambitions he forfeited something precious, he leaves the ball park and wanders sadly into the Denver night.

Elsewhere in Kerouac's fiction, though, there are lyrical depictions of childhood sandlot baseball games, games in which the narrator, Jack Duluoz, becomes wholly engrossed in the moment, the motion, the flow and unfolding of a play, fully absorbed, fully focused and fully present, attaining a state of self-transcending attentiveness and of communion with his team-mates: "at supper summer dusk we rushed out for games of scrub and sometimes double play right on the diamond ... high grass waved in the redness, Lousy piped from third base, flung me the double play ball, I pivoted on a hinch and flung around back to first with a hitch and dip of my shoulders and a whomp into first high hard straight, Scotty at short on the next tap scoops up his grasscutter ... holds the ball gravely in his meat hand before I know it and is slipping me a softie over the keystone which I have to come in charging synchronized with the Scotty ball a foot off ground which I do with meat hand and still running (and with passing foot-tap at sack) flick under my left side with all my might to join the first baseman's mitt with my straightline loop of reasoning hurl." [34] At such moments of complete engagement in the game self-conscious selfhood is suspended and there is neither room nor time in the mind for vanity.

Another significant baseball incident occurs in the novel, *Maggie Cassidy*. [35] Here, the young high school centerfielder, Jack Duluoz, relates in delighted detail the circumstances of his having made an exceptional catch, a play that exceeds the usual limit of his capacities: "I ran over from the soft new grass clods and slanted and got behind O'Higgins in his own left field (from my center) and tapped the ground till that ball from high heaven came slowing down and hugening for the ground arc over my head – I reached the backhand glove and got it running away from the plate ... I brought it down almost stumbling, tucking it in my belly, O'Higgins was not sure what I had just done behind, I heard Larsen Whoop! at the fungo bat – Beautiful catch, beautiful spring – ." In making such a play there is in the mind of the player a sense of having partaken of an act of grace, a poetry of motion invisibly inscribed in time, a sense of being part maker, part recipient of an Act of Beauty.

The novel *Desolation Angels* finds the now 34 year old Jack Duluoz working as a Fire Lookout for the National Forest Service, living alone in a small cabin atop a remote mountain peak. On lonely summer evenings in his hermitage, Duluoz finds solace in playing by lantern light his self-invented fantasy baseball game: "I shuffle my deck, write out the lineups, and lay out the teams – For hundreds of miles around, black night." [36] Every inning, every play, every player is vividly, meticulously imagined, every statistic duly recorded. An affecting, haunting image: a game of baseball played entirely in the mind of a lonely man at night in a remote wilderness cabin.

When in September, at the end of his season atop Desolation Peak, Duluoz returns to the life of the world, among the first things he does is to buy a copy of *Sporting News* to read in his skidrow hotel room, spending "an hour and a half in my room ... reading about Mickey Mantle and the Three-I League and the Southern Association and the West Texas League and the latest trades and stars and kids upcoming and even reading the Little League news to see the names of the 10-year old prodigy pitchers." [37]

Scattered among Kerouac's other writings are references to baseball, bearing various thematic implications. In *Tristessa,* the narrator, bleakly brooding on our common human misapprehension of the nature of reality and on the futility of human endeavour in the world, observes in the crowded night streets of Mexico City the young "winners of tonight's ballgame." Walking home elated with victory, secretly each boy feels uncertain, wondering to himself: "Did I make a bad play in the fifth inning? Didn't I make it up with that *heet* in the seventh inning?" [38] Victory in this world, the vignette suggests, is forever insufficient, forever elusive, forever illusory.

Like spirits of the blessèd, baseball players pass through Kerouac's poems. Smiling and floating through the bright blue skies of Paradise, Roy Campanella makes an appearance in Kerouac's lyric, "Heaven." [39] In *Old Angel Midnight,* from out of a murky blur of words and sounds, four other immortals of the game of baseball come suddenly and sharply into view: "Bobby Mathews of Philadelphia & Ed Crane of NY accomplished the feat before 1900 (striking out four men in 1 inning) – O those old ballgames, O lost Foleys of South Boston in old time Boston raw drump drunk days I love you – Geo Hooks Wiltse of the Giants did it on May 15, 1906 ..." [40] Even in the rush and flux and hubbub of insubstantial, ephemeral reality, as represented in *Old Angel Midnight,* certain notable achievements still stand as beacons or guideposts.

Baseball is also the subject of two other poems by Jack Kerouac – two untitled free-verse haiku written in the 1950s. Indeed, Kerouac is credited with being the originator of the American baseball haiku, which has since become a genre in itself within that poetic form. [41] Kerouac's two baseball haiku bookend the baseball season. [42] The first of the two is set in the spring:

Empty baseball field –
A robin,
Hops along the bench

There are two incisive commentaries on this poem, the first made by Cor van den Heuvel, one of the editors of the anthology, *Baseball Haiku,* and another made by Chen-ou Liu on his blog, *Never Ending Story.* Van den Heuvel writes: "Though this haiku does not directly present aspects of the game itself, Kerouac manages to evoke a combination of feelings that we can associate with the game. First there is the lonely feeling called up by the emptiness of the field, then the contrasting sense of promise provided by the entrance of the robin – a sign of spring indicating that ball players will also soon appear on the field." [43] Using the abbreviations "L1" for line one of the poem and "Ls 2&3" for lines two and three, Chen-ou Liu observes that "L1 sets the context, seasonal, thematic and emotive, while allusive Ls 2&3 make a shift in theme and imagery, thus establishing a contrasting relationship with their preceding line through Kerouac's skilful use of the zoom-in technique. This contrasting relationship fully embodies the 'principle of internal comparison' which is well articulated by Harold G. Henderson in his study of Japanese haiku (p.18) therefore it gains added poignancy.

Kerouac's two-axis, cinematic haiku is beautifully crafted and serves well as a starting point for many thoughts and emotions." [44]

Kerouac's second baseball haiku is nearly classical in its observations of the poetic conventions of the form: set in the present, making reference to the season, to nature and to a particular event, as well as deploying a pregnant omission or suggestive ellipsis.

> How cold!
> – late September
> baseball –
> the crickets

In plain language and concrete sensual imagery (cold, crickets) this short, resonant poem expresses sad anticipation of the end of the baseball season, together with an underlying sense of melancholy and loss at the imminent autumnal decline. (A reminder that life is brief, time is fleeting.) As the summer warmth now gives way to early autumn chill, the life that spring brought forth is ending. Like baseball, crickets (poor, hapless creatures) are born in the spring, come to maturity during the summer and die in the fall, all their chirping at an end.

The theme implied here would seem to be that of life's transience.

"Ronnie on the Mound," a short-story by Kerouac first published in *Esquire* in 1958, is a more compressed, more proficient treatment of a motif originally dealt with by the author in "Raw Rookie Nerves," – a young player's initiatory ordeal in his first major league game. [45] The narrative describes a decisive episode in the career of a promising 19 year old pitcher, Ronnie Melaney, who has just been called up from the minors to the Pittsburgh Plymouths. In his first game for his new team he takes the mound in the first inning of a crucial game against the Chicago Chryslers (both teams part of Kerouac's private fantasy baseball leagues.) The whole of the story's action consists of the events of the top half of the first inning as Melaney debuts, faltering, failing, losing confidence, recovering, summoning just enough skill and steadfastness to scrape through the inning.

Awkward and ragged as his debut with the Plymouths proves to be, Melaney succeeds in completing his rite-of-passage. He has discovered the gap between hope and fulfilment and learned that sheer perseverance in the face of adversity and uncertainty can be as valuable on the mound as a good pitching repertoire. His harrow-ing first inning has also served as a lesson in perspective – on himself, on the game and its demands, and on life. "Only one out and two to go," he reflects grimly at one point, "then only one inning and eight to go, and then one game and thirty, forty for the year, and then only one year and twenty to go (if lucky) and then death O Lord." [46]

In the conclusion of the story the third-person narrator states that though chastened and deflated, the young pitcher is not defeated: Ronnie, he pronounces, "is made" as a player. Kerouac is adept here at portraying Ronnie's sensations, thoughts and emotions, but also at rendering in vivid vernacular the play-by-play subtleties of the game and, not least, in evoking the ambience of a game of baseball played on a soft spring evening with the feel of a cool breeze moving across the field, the smell of tobacco smoke wafting from the stands, the calls of beer sellers and hot dog vendors, the murmur of fans arriving late, youngsters yelling in the bleachers, the bright lamps of the stadium. "Ronnie on the Mound" is a lively and engaging paean to the deeper meanings of the game and its power and poetry.

In the late 1950s and early 1960s, under the collective title of *The Last Word,* Kerouac wrote a series of columns (informal, personal essays, written in a conversational style) for the magazine, *Escapade.* His column for the July

1959 issue of the magazine takes as its subject the author's views on the current state of baseball. [47]

In a mood of annoyance and in tones of disapproval, Kerouac poses to readers a series of rhetorical questions all with the aim of criticizing what he sees as misguided interventions by self-appointed experts in the practices and performances of players: batting stances, use of specialized equipment, infield shifts, and other tactical calculations. In defense of what he views as traditional "honest baseball," the author deplores "silly trickery," "master-minding" and micro-managing by a host of planning, advising, controlling, interfering "know-it-alls," including theorists, consultants, owners, managers and general managers. Kerouac extols, instead, what is instinctive and individual in a player, the following of ones own self-discovered natural bent. He favors a spirited, spontaneous approach to the game, commending zest over artifice, organic form over mechanic form. "Let there be joy in baseball again," he enjoins. [48]

Kerouac's conception of original energies and aptitudes in players that should be fostered rather than contorted and stunted by experts has significant parallels to that principle referred to in Taoism as "the uncarved block," that is to say wood "in its natural condition, uncarved and unpainted ... symbol of man's natural state, when his inborn powers have not been tampered with." [49] Each player performing according to his individual essence, acting in the spirit of unmediated self-expression (free of external manipulations and meddlings) would – in Kerouac's view – serve to reinstate and elevate the game, keeping alive in it something vital and life-giving.

The attitudes concerning contemporary baseball expressed in *The Last Word* column for July 1959 are consistent with the affirmation of individuality that is central to nearly all of Kerouac's writing. He cherishes independence of mind and spirit, admires distinctive, vivid characters, and deprecates all those forces and agencies that seek to iron out variety and oddity in the world. In "On the Origins of a Generation," the essay in which he wrote with esteem of Ted Williams and Bobby Thomson, the author laments what he perceives to be the current waning of an America that was formerly "invested with wild selfbelieving individuality." [50] Kerouac views baseball as a stronghold of and a sanctuary for certain kinds of eccentric individuals, men indifferent to prim and priggish social mores, men content to be themselves, living according to their own inclinations, behaving with careless unconventionality. Invented names of players from the rosters of Kerouac's fantasy baseball teams confirm the author's habitual liking for raffish, raucous types, for mavericks and free spirits: "Wino" Love, "Hophead" Dean, "Bop" Walters, "Alky" Anderson and others. In the argot of the Beat era, it will be remembered, "wild" was a term of approbation, synonymous with excellent. The word signified all that was not subdued by convention and authority, all that remains natural, original and genuine. It is this essential quality of the game of baseball that in his *Last Word* column Kerouac seeks to defend against what he sees as the overbearing theoreticians and engineers of the game, those he characterizes as "know-it-alls" and whom he fears are determined to flatten the quirks and singularities of the players, robbing baseball (and the nation) of color and authenticity.

Jack Kerouac's actual last (published) word on baseball took the form of a newspaper column titled "In Mid-June My Ideas About the Major League Race," which appeared in the St. Petersburg, Florida *Evening Independent* on June 16, 1965. [51] As Kerouac was later to explain to his bibliographer, commenting on the piece: "That's on the baseball pennant race for that year. I picked Tigers and Milwaukee Braves, was wrong." [52]

There is a notable difference in tone between Kerouac's critical 1959 *Last Word* column and his 1965 piece in the *Evening Independent.* In the latter, Kerouac evinces eager enjoyment in the unfolding baseball season and is generous in his praise of the players. Briefly but shrewdly, he evaluates the infield, outfield and pitching staff of the Detroit Tigers in the American League and the Milwaukee Braves in the National League. Clearly, he has been following a lot of games, so his assessments are informed. Kerouac concludes his column (and thus three decades of intermittent writings on baseball) by citing and endorsing a statement he attributes to Jay Hanna "Dizzy" Dean: "Ain't nothing I like better than a good ballgame."

It is clear that baseball exercised a powerful hold over Kerouac's imagination. It was for him an activity charged with significance, a felt connection to something vital and meaningful. At various times in his writing the game takes on different meanings – a place of refreshment and renewal, a source of life-lessons and of inspiration, a vehicle for self-examination and self-transcendence, a sanctuary for what is genuine and humanly heroic in the world. And, it is noteworthy that although in his youth Kerouac excelled at football, winning with his skills a scholarship to Columbia University, throughout his writings it is baseball he treats in tender recollection; it is baseball that brightened his inward glooms, and that – in the form of self-invented fantasy baseball – sustained him in his solitary hours.

In Kerouac's novel of adolescence, *Maggie Cassidy*, the narrator describes how during the winter months the boys in his gang of friends look forward to the coming of spring and Opening Day and how in bleak winter streets they play "imaginary catch" and mime pitches in anticipation of the baseball season. [53] In contrast, in *Vanity of Duluoz*, the narrator recalls "the awful blood-flying games" of football he and his adolescent friends engaged in: "These later sandlot games were so awful I was afraid to get up on Saturday mornings and show up." [54] Later, playing college football, the narrator is knocked uncon-scious in one game, while during a later game: "I hear a loud crack and it's my leg breaking." [55]

A pastoral game, far gentler than football and played at a leisurely pace, baseball serves for many as a refuge from the ravening world, an intimation, even, of a more ideal world, a world (as old Omar Khayyam says) "nearer to the heart's desire." Baseball, the scholar and theologian Gregory K. Hillis has written: "has the eternal built into it, from the circular nature of each player's voyage around the base paths to its refusal to have the game limited by the constraints of time." [56] And is there not also something of the eternal suggested by the undefined and thus ulti-mately unlimited dimensions of a baseball park? As the Pulitzer Prize winning author and architect, Paul

Goldberger has noted: "In both time and space it's technically infinite. It's the only major team sport that's not played against the clock ... [and] the outfield could go on forever in theory." [57] David Bentley Hart is of a similar opinion: "All its configurations and movements aspire to the timeless and the boundless." [58]

Whether performed on a diamond or in the mind, baseball was for Kerouac a bright elsewhere, an autonomous precinct of grace and beauty, a haven for the heart. Played under open skies, on lush spring and summer grass, remote from ever-running, rushing time and with outfields extending into infinity, baseball must have seemed to him both the evocation of an unfallen world and a hint of heaven. These, surely, may be seen to lend to the game a measure of holiness.

NOTES

---

[1] *Pull My Daisy, Text by Jack Kerouac for the Film by Robert Frank and Alfred Leslie,* New York: Grove Press, 1961, p. 25 & p. 30.

[2] "Baseball and the American Dream" by George Grella, *The Massachusetts Review,* Vol. 16, No. 3 (Summer 1975) p. 551.

[3] *Ibid.* p. 552.

[4] "Ritual in the Church of Baseball" by Michael L. Butterworth, *Communication and Critical/Cultural Studies,* Vol. 2, No. 2 (June 2005) p. 107.

[5] "Is Baseball Sacred?" by Gary Laderman, *Huffpost*, 10 April 2013. https://www.huffpost.com/entry/is-baseball-sacred_b_3033183

[6] "A Perfect Game: The Metaphysical Meaning of Baseball" by David Bentley Hunt, *First Things,* August 2010 at firstthings.com/article/2010/08/a-perfect-game

[7] *Ibid.*

[8] *Baseball as a Road to God* by John Sexton, Avery/Random House, New York, 2014.

[9] *Ibid.* p. 177.

[10] *Ibid.* p. 215.

[11] *Ibid.* p. 215.

[12] *Baseball Metaphysics* by Daniel McNeil, Independently Published, 2019, pp. 19-20.

[13] *Baseball as Metaphysics* by Marvin Cohen, Arlington, Massachusetts, Tough Poets Press, 2017, p. 89.

[14] *Ibid.*

[15] *Ibid.* p. 99.

[16] *Ibid.* p. 60.

[17] *Ibid.* pp. 103-104.

[18] *Collected Poems 1953-1993* by John Updike, Alfred A. Knopf, New York, 1993, p. 8.

[19] *Kerouac at Bat: Fantasy Sports and the King of the Beats* by Isaac Gewirtz, New York: The New York Public Library, 2009. See also Stan Isaac's account of playing fantasy baseball with Kerouac: *Newsday* February 17, 1961, reprinted online as "A Strange Game of Baseball with a Legendary Writer" at http://www.thecolumnists.com/isaacs/isaacs69.html

[20] *Atop an Underwood* by Jack Kerouac, edited with an introduction and commentary by Paul Marion, New York, Viking, 1999.

[21] *Ibid.* p.17.

[22] "Every intentional action, such as the hitting of a baseball, would also include the act of deciding to hit the baseball." Page 26 of *Free*

Will: A Contemporary Introduction by Michael McKenna & Derek Pereboom, Routledge, New York: 2016.

[23] *Atop an Underwood,* p. 17.

[24] "Journal 1951" by Jack Kerouac in *The Unknown Kerouac,* edited by Todd Tietchen, The Library of America, New York: 2016, p. 134.

[25] *Ibid.*

[26] *Ibid.*

[27] *Ibid.*
[28] "On the Origins of a Generation" by Jack Kerouac, *Playboy,* Vol. VI , No. 6, June 1959, pp. 31-32, 42, 79. Reprinted in *Good Blonde & Others* by Jack Kerouac, edited by Donald Allen, San Francisco: Grey Fox Press, 1993, pp. 55 – 65.

[29] *Ibid.* p. 64.

[30] *Ibid.* p. 63.

[31] "He was BEAT – the root, the soul of Beatific." *On the Road* by Jack Kerouac, Viking Press, New York, 1957, p. 195.

[32] *Ibid.* pp- 252-253.

[33] *Ibid.* p. 181.

[34] *Dr. Sax* by Jack Kerouac, Grove Press, New York, 1959, p. 53.

[35] *Maggie Cassidy* by Jack Kerouac, Avon Books, New York, 1959, p. 151.

[36] *Desolation Angels* by Jack Kerouac, Coward-McCann, New York, 1965, pp. 13 -16.

[37] *Ibid.* p. 104.

[38] *Tristessa* by Jack Kerouac, Avon Books, New York, 1960, p. 55.

[39] "Heaven" in *Heaven & Other Poems* by Jack Kerouac, Grey Fox Press, Bolinas, Ca. 1977, p. 28.

[40] *Old Angel Midnight* by Jack Kerouac, Grey Fox Press, San Francisco, 1993, p. 18.

[41] "The first American baseball haiku was written by Jack Kerouac." *Introduction: Warming Up* by Cor van den Heuvel *Baseball Haiku:The Best Haiku Ever Written About The Game,* edited by Cor van den Heuvel & Nanae Tamura, Norton & Co. New York, 2007, p. *xxvii.*

[42] The two untitled haiku are to be found in *Book of Haikus* by Jack Kerouac, edited with an introduction by Regina Weinreich, New York & London, Penguin Books, 2003, p. 27, p. 168.

[43] *Baseball Haiku,* p. *xxix.*

[44] *Never Ending Story: First English-Chinese Bilingual Haiku and Tanka Blog,* by Chen-ou Liu, Friday, March 21, 2014, at neverendingstoryhaikutankablogspot.com/2014/03/poetic-musings-first-baseball-haiku-by.html

[45] "Ronnie on the Mound" by Jack Kerouac, *Esquire* Vol. XLIX, No. 5, May 1958, pp. 87-88. Reprinted in *Good Blonde & Others,* pp. 139-46.

[46] *Ibid.* p. 143.

[47] "The Last Word," by Jack Kerouac, *Escapade* (July 1959) reprinted in *Good Blonde & Others,* pp. 162-65.

[48] *Ibid.* p. 165.

[49] *Three Ways of Thought in Ancient China* by Arthur Waley, Allen & Unwin, London, 1939, p. 96.

[50] "On the Origins of the Beat Generation" in *Good Blonde & Others,* p. 59.

[51] "In Mid-June My Ideas About the Major League Race" by Jack Kerouac, St. Petersburg, Florida *Evening Independent,* June 16, 1965. Reprinted in *Good Blonde & Others,* pp. 146-47.

[52] *A Bibliography of Works by Jack Kerouac,* compiled by Ann Charters, Phoenix, Bookshop, New York, 1967, p. 63.

[53] *Maggie Cassidy,* p. 116.

[54] *Vanity of Duluoz* by Jack Kerouac, Coward.McCann, New York, 1968, p. 14.

[55] *Ibid.* p. 74.

---

[56] *"Quit Trying to Fix Baseball"* by Gregory K. Hillis, *Commonweal* 27 March 2018, commonwealmagazine.org/quit-trying-fix-baseball

[57] "Tanner Howard Interviews Paul Goldberger, author of *Ballpark: Baseball in the American City"* deadspin.com/the-ballpark-is-the-great-american space-1834566170

[58] "A Perfect Game: The Metaphysical Meaning of Baseball" by David Bentley Hart, *op cit.*